Original title:

Through the Island Fog

Copyright © 2025 Creative Arts Management OÜ
All rights reserved.

Author: Miriam Kensington
ISBN HARDBACK: 978-1-80581-657-7
ISBN PAPERBACK: 978-1-80581-184-8
ISBN EBOOK: 978-1-80581-657-7

The Lure of the Hazy Horizon

A sailor once lost his snack,
He swore it slipped right from his pack.
The gulls all giggled, quite a sight,
As chips and dips took off in flight.

With every wave that crashed nearby,
He wondered just how seagulls fly.
Round and round like dancers they twirl,
While he just sat, a hungry girl.

Reflections and Reveries in Soft Grey

A fisherman dropped his shiny lure,
It danced away, a crafty tour.
"Come back, you slippery little spark!"
He muttered darkly, lost in the dark.

His net was full of seaweed's cheer,
But all the fish just disappeared.
In puns and laughter he found glee,
For sea life thrives on a mystery.

Lost Footprints on the Misty Path

Footprints led to nowhere near,
A muddy squish, a slip, a cheer.
In foggy depths, they tangled round,
And shuffle-step became the sound.

A walker tripped on friendly slime,
"Is this an art, or just a crime?"
With giggles echoing through the trees,
Each step became a joke with ease.

The Enchantment of Obscured Light

The sun peeked shyly through the haze,
It played hide-and-seek in clever ways.
With shadows dancing on the ground,
It turned the day upside down.

A crab in costume waved his claws,
While tourists laughed and dropped their jaws.
"What's that?" they shouted with delight,
While crabs just giggled at the sight.

The Vanishing Point

In a world so blurred and gray,
I lost my keys, they skedaddled away.
A penguin laughs as it waddles past,
I swear they were right here, not vanished so fast!

A crab runs by with a sneaky grin,
Is he my thief or where do I begin?
The fog keeps thickening, my plans go askew,
Did I leave them on the last hill I flew?

Shadows of Time

Ghosts dance around, in funny attire,
Telling tales of when they played with fire.
They trip and they tumble, what a sight to see,
When the past gets lost in ancient jubilee!

I asked them their secret, they chuckled away,
They said, "Time is stretchy, it's a game we play!"
Then one lost his shoe and the other his hat,
They danced in the shadows, how 'bout that?

Faded Footprints

Footprints leading to the quirkier shore,
Each one a tale of the slips and the more.
With every step taken, a giggle's revealed,
A duck in a tutu, who knew it would yield?

The wind whispers secrets, the tide starts to laugh,
As a crab chases seagulls on an ocean path.
Faded trails of wonder, what was once a face,
Now blurry with laughter in this giggly place!

Forgotten Shores

On shores where laughter meets ground without plan,
A beach ball's bursting, do I want to ran?
With dolphins giggling and seagulls in flight,
We're all just caught up in this whimsical plight!

Sandcastles tumble, we cheer with delight,
Each bucket of laughter turns wrong into right.
"Oh dear!" shouts a crab, "We've lost the sun!"
But it's just a mischief, we're here for the fun!

Isle of Dreams

On the shores where seagulls dance,
Waves whisper secrets, a merry prance.
I tripped on seaweed, oh what a sight,
Fell in the tide, what a fishy fight!

Sandcastles built with dreams and glee,
But I found a crab, not a cup of tea.
It waved a claw, I laughed out loud,
No royalty here, just a crustacean crowd.

Twilight Over Water

The sun dips low, a comical show,
Fish are giggling, don't you know?
A lighthouse with eyes, blinking in jest,
"Time for the party!" it shouts, not at rest.

Fireflies join in, like stars on a spree,
They dance with the breeze, wild and free.
A frog jumps high, slips into the lake,
Ribbiting laughter, oh what a mistake!

Unraveled Mysteries

The trees are whispering, secrets galore,
Unraveling yarns of creatures that snore.
A raccoon in pajamas, quite the odd sight,
Stealing snacks by the pale moonlight.

A shell sings softly, "I'm quite a catch!"
But it's only a seat for a crab and a hatch.
Layers of laughs in each twist and turn,
A mystery of mirth—oh, how I yearn!

Solace in the Softness

In the soft embrace of evening's tease,
A turtle strolls with comical ease.
It stops for a snack, a leaf so grand,
"Fast food!" it yells, waving its hand.

The stars giggle down, twinkling bright,
They wink at the moon, what a silly sight.
A breeze tickles leaves, making them chuckle,
Nature's own stand-up, a fun little shuffle.

Dancing with Shadows

Beneath the veil of hazy grey,
My feet stumble in a merry ballet.
I trip over tags of my own shoes,
Those shadows laugh, I dance out the blues.

They twirl and spin with the brightest flair,
Yet vanish quick, leaving naught but air.
The moon peers down in a cheeky grin,
In this foggy hall, I lose and win.

Breaths of the Damp Air

In the thick mist, I take a whiff,
Of something strange—it's my old gym sniff!
I wave my arms like a seasoned chef,
Trying to season the fog—what a mess!

Each breath I take feels rather odd,
Did I inhale a wet sock or a cod?
I coughed and wheezed, yet laughed out loud,
In this flavor a fog's never proud.

Traces of Forgotten Steps

With every step, I dance with fate,
Muddy footprints lead me to a plate.
Where's the pies I smell? Oh, what a tease,
Instead, I find my lost left shoe with ease!

I skip around, trying to find my grace,
Yet the fog is a trickster, it loves to chase.
I'll leave my mark like breadcrumbs tossed,
A trail of laughter, with no path lost.

The Cloaked Wanderer

A figure cloaked, with a hat so wide,
He ducks and dives, trying to hide.
But wait! It's just my neighbor's dog,
In shadows thick, looking for the bog.

"Oh, good day, Mister Fog of War,
Or is that just a mischievous door?"
With snorts and barks, he leads the way,
An adventure born from foggy play!

Veils of Mist

In the morning, gnomes roam,
Lost in a foggy dome.
They trip on seaweed strands,
And proclaim they've found lands!

A seagull steals a hat,
While a crab plans a chat.
Shells gather for a dance,
And the sand crabs take a chance.

Soon a lighthouse gives a frown,
As the foam pulls it down.
Waves laugh at the joke,
While the dolphins start to poke.

At last, the sun breaks free,
But where's my cup of tea?
With a wink the fog rolls out,
And the seagulls cheer and shout.

Shadows at Dawn

Tall trees join the parade,
In misty masquerade.
Squirrels with sunglasses cheer,
While the raccoons throw beer!

A turtle gets the fright,
From a shadow in flight.
Just a puffin in disguise,
With a wink and funny eyes.

Sea turtles trade their shells,
For tales and ocean smells.
Echoes of laughter ring,
As willow trees start to sing.

When the sun clears the way,
They laugh at yesterday.
Foggy antics vanish quick,
When the light comes with a tick.

Whispering Tides

The tides tell secrets low,
While the starfish start to glow.
Jellyfish dress for a ball,
While the seaweed takes a fall.

A gull with popcorn pride,
Takes a seat on a tide.
While crabs hold a debate,
About who's the best plate!

Waves tease the sandy shore,
And the barnacles implore.
Clams peek from their shells wide,
With a wink and foolish pride.

Ahoy to all that play,
With a splash, they bounce away.
As the fog begins to clear,
Laughter is what we hear!

Secrets of the Shore

Seashells reveal their tales,
Of pirate ships and gales.
An octopus cracks a joke,
As the sand dollars folk choke.

Seagulls mimic a sax,
While crabs learn to relax.
The waves do a soft jig,
While starfish dance a gig!

The driftwood holds a seer,
Whispering, "Have no fear!"
With every wave of cheer,
The beach ball draws near.

But as the day turns bright,
They trade what feels just right.
For when the fog drifts away,
All fun is here to stay!

Navigating Dreams Amidst Haze

Woke up to find my socks on the cat,
The kettle's dancing, imagine that!
A compass spins, where am I now?
Chasing shadows, I'll take a bow.

Every step's a wobbly guess,
Is this a party or just a mess?
I trip on visions of giggling gnomes,
In this fog of misfit homes.

With every turn, I lose my way,
But the seagulls laugh in their own play.
This dream is wacky, bright and loud,
Yet somehow, I'm still quite proud.

So here in haze, I'll take my stand,
Waltzing with my invisible band.
Life's a laugh, even when it's bleak,
Give me fog and a funny streak.

Fragments of Memory in Damp Air

Frogs wear hats, or so I think,
In this mist, there's always a wink.
A clock chimes backwards, what a thrill,
Time runs wild, like a cartoon spill.

My lost keys dance in a puddle of hope,
With umbrellas made of bubble tape.
I meet a crab who tells a joke,
But only laughs when I say 'coke.'

Wet whispers swirl in silvery streams,
Telling tall tales from childhood dreams.
A jellyfish juggles, to my surprise,
While seaweed sways to the gulls' cries.

In the damp air, all logic's a game,
My thoughts long foggy and rather lame.
Yet with chuckles and giggles, I find my bliss,
In fragments of memory, can't say I miss.

Of Oysters and Illusions in the Fog

Oysters grin with pearls in sight,
Telling tales of their underwater night.
A clam and a shrimp pull off a show,
While the tide claps and moves to and fro.

"Is this a dream?" the oyster asks,
As a fish in a tuxedo performs odd tasks.
The bubbles giggle; it's quite absurd,
What's true and false, really, who's heard?

The seaweed twirls, boasts a dance,
While a starfish winks, given the chance.
Mystery lurks with a wink of a eye,
Where the shrimp makes pasta, oh my, oh my!

Mirthful madness cloaked in this spray,
Where oysters laugh at the dull day.
A foggy escape with laughter abound,
Is it real, or just what I found?

Secrets of the Sea, Half-Seen

Secrets swim beneath the foam,
A crab's bizarrely woven home.
Half-seen wonders drift and prance,
Like jellybeans in a crazy dance.

A squid spills ink, not with a frown,
Sketching mermaids in a fashion gown.
Turtles gossip, oh, what a scene,
While fish wear glasses, you've never seen.

The whispers of shells, secrets galore,
"Who's the fairest? Who wants more?"
A dolphin jokes, flips with flair,
Shows off his bubble-filledchair.

Beneath the laughs, the sea is bright,
With half-seen dreams, it's a whimsical sight.
So let's dive down, without a care,
In the depths of folly, let's float and share.

The Masked Horizon

In a haze where ducks will float,
I lost my hat and my red coat.
Seagulls laugh as I chase a call,
Every step, I stumble, then I fall.

Fog rolls in with a ghostly dance,
My socks are wet, but I'll take a chance.
A crab in a tuxedo bids me hi,
"Can you keep a secret?" it whispers sly.

Mermaids giggle from far-off shores,
While I search for a pair of missing oars.
Under misty skies, laughter swells,
As I slip on seaweed and ring their bells.

Yet at dusk, when the shadows play,
I'll charm the fog to lead my way.
With a grin and a wave from the tide,
I'll dance with the laughter, my trusty guide.

Tides of Memory

Waves crash loud like a piñata's cheer,
Bringing back tales I forgot to hear.
Beneath the surf, old shoes do leap,
I trip on shells, laughing, in deep.

Napping crabs wear glasses too,
Sipping tea, they shout, "How do you do?"
A fish with a hat hoots with delight,
As I lose the beach ball in the night.

Seashell music plays a silly tune,
Dancing to the grumpy moon.
With a wink, the tide gives a push,
And I take a dive, with a happy hush.

In memory's ebb, I find the fun,
Each wave a hug, my race is done.
So here I'll stay, in this playful plot,
Forever lost, but laughing a lot.

Realm of the Shrouded

In the mist where giggles hide,
A lobster rides a excited tide.
"Are you lost?" a wise old seal,
I replied, "Do you have a meal?"

The horizon dims, but spirits soar,
As laughs echo from the ocean floor.
Surfboards glide on a ghostly swell,
Summoning tales I can't quite tell.

Frogs in top hats do a jig,
While I try not to step on their gig.
Silly dances in the drizzling rain,
Each misstep a comedy, oh what a gain!

In a realm where nonsense reigns,
The fogworn paths are full of gains.
With every chuckle, I lose my way,
Here in jest, forever I'll play.

Melodies in the Mist

A foggy serenade whispers low,
As I stumble on rocks shaped like a toe.
Tunes from the waves wrap me tight,
While giggly dolphins take to flight.

Nonsense trees wear scarves and caps,
As I join in their misty laps.
Juggling sea cucumbers, what a sight,
Under the stars sparkling at night.

Sandcastles sing with a silly sound,
Dancing crabs all gathered around.
In the shroud, everything's a jest,
Each laugh a journey, never a quest.

So let the breezes pull at my hair,
In this whimsical world, without a care.
With every chuckle, the night becomes bright,
Melodies escaping with pure delight.

Liminal Spaces

In the mist, the crabs do dance,
With a sideways jig, they take their chance.
A seagull squawks, wearing a hat,
As the saltiest breeze gives a gentle spat.

Lost my keys in the swirling gray,
Even a fish takes a moment to stay.
I swear a mermaid just winked at me,
Oh wait, that's just a plastic sea debris.

Muffled laughter floats through the haze,
Guided by echoes of old, silly days.
Whispers of fish tales fill the air,
While I trip on a rock—oh look, a chair!

Here we stand, in these layers of fun,
Where the sun peeks out like a playful gun.
Every wave holds its own little prank,
Floating thoughts, drifting like a tank.

Fogsw swept Memories

Fog rolls in with a cheeky grin,
Ducking and weaving, let the games begin.
Lost my shoe to a wave's surprise,
Turns out it's just a crab wearing my size.

Old time sailors, their tales untold,
Swapping their stories like treasures of gold.
I heard one claim his ghost ship's near,
But it's just my lunch floating on beer.

As I step on a jelly, it wobbles quite wide,
What's lurking beneath? A big fish with pride.
Laughter erupts from the dense greenery,
Nature's stand-up, full of mystery.

Waves tickle toes with a playful jest,
With every splash, the world feels blessed.
Memories wrapped in the salty air,
In this fog, we lighten our cares.

The Unseen Landscape

The world is gray, but oh, what a sight,
A raccoon in shadows, stealing a bite.
It stumbles and fumbles, gives me a scare,
Only to trip on a seaweed chair.

I call it a boat—my soda can craft,
Drifting with style, what a goofy raft.
The gulls are giggling, in on the joke,
As a fisherman frowns at my bubbly yoke.

Peering out, there's a path to explore,
Where everything's funny, like never before.
Muffled whispers share secrets of fun,
As a seal flips fish like his day's just begun.

In the low light, odd shapes bounce and glide,
With hues of absurdity blooping wide.
Steering through giggles, on waves we ride,
In this unseen world, where joys collide.

Enigma of the Tide

Tides pull at troubles, like socks missing pairs,
What's lost in the surf is found in the airs.
A sea cucumber waves, quite preposterous,
I laugh at the thought—this life's quite comical.

Puddles of laughter splash on the ground,
While seaweed wiggles, with humor abound.
Even the driftwood has stories to tell,
Of tipsy thrashings and pots made of shell.

Each wave rolls in with a legendary spin,
While the ocean grins like it knows where we've been.
Seashells are clapping, right there on the shore,
For all of our blunders, they always want more.

In the ebb and the flow, a dance we create,
Where the sea meets the land, we celebrate.
Chasing horizons with chuckles, let's glide,
In the enigma, where laughter won't hide.

The Haunting Calm

In the mist, a seagull squawks,
Looking for lost socks.
A crab with a top hat strolls,
While jellyfish play with shoals.

Ghostly trees tiptoe around,
Whispers of laughter abound.
A whale strums a ukulele,
Making sure it's all cheery.

Serenade of the Sea

The fish hold a disco ball,
Swirls of color, what a ball!
Crabs dance in their funky shoes,
A party where you can't lose.

Waves tap to the beat so sweet,
A chorus of splashes and feet.
Mermaids juggling fish like pro,
While dolphins steal the show!

Lurking Hopes

In the fog, a treasure map,
X marks where dreams take a nap.
A pirate with a rubber duck,
His plans are just pure luck.

Turtles playing hide and seek,
Whispering secrets unique.
A parrot tends a bean plant,
Singing songs, oh so gallant!

Nebulous Journeys

Clouds ride on fluffy chairs,
Sharing jokes with the sea bears.
A compass spins like a top,
No telling when it will stop.

Boats bouncing like on a trampoline,
Chasing dreams, oh so serene.
A fish dons a sailor's cap,
Ready for a funny mishap.

Secrets Beneath the Salty Veil

Beneath the waves where secrets hide,
A crab in shades plays truth or lied.
He sneaks a peek at fish in gowns,
While seagulls giggle with silly frowns.

The oysters boast of pearls, so grand,
But one thinks sand's a tasty brand.
The clams just chime in with a wink,
And all agree they're on the brink.

Jellyfish dance like they're so slick,
While seaweed sways to a jazzy tick.
The tide rolls in, the tide rolls out,
While fish are plotting what life's about.

As sunsets glow in colors bold,
The sea whispers tales of fortune told.
With every wave, laughter reigns,
In this salty kingdom where joy remains.

Shadows on the Tidal Edge

The shadows creep as night takes hold,
Crabs in capes, feeling quite bold.
They prance about in a goofy line,
While the moon laughs softly, feeling divine.

A starfish dreams of becoming a star,
Wishing on shells from his pebbly bar.
The octopus rolls out of bed,
He juggles fish, but they all fled!

On the shore, the pelicans dive,
With hopes of catching a feast alive.
But with every splash and silly dunk,
They just end up with a stinky trunk.

As the tide teases with each retreat,
The shadows dance, a rhythmic beat.
With laughter echoing through the night,
It's a party here, oh what a sight!

Dreams Adrift in Shrouded Waters

The fog rolls in, like whipped cream fluff,
Where fish wear hats, it's never tough.
They gather 'round for a fishy chat,
Debating if dolphins are dogs or cats!

With bubbles rising like giggles afloat,
A mermaid's tale becomes quite the joke.
She sings of treasure and golden sands,
While the sea turtles plan their rock bands.

Waves whisper softly, teasing the shore,
As crabs consult maps they can't ignore.
"Where's the fish fry?" they ask with glee,
As seagulls mock, "That's lost at sea!"

In this watery world of whimsy and play,
Every glance is a smirk in a silly way.
They dream of the land with its bright shiny rays,
But laugh 'neath the waves for their salty ways.

Echoes of Solitude at Dawn

At dawn, the shadows start to yawn,
While clams play chess on the wet, cool lawn.
The sun peeks in, with a cheeky grin,
And fishes giggle as day begins.

With gentle waves playing hide and seek,
A starfish cracks jokes that are quite unique.
He tells of days when the tide was high,
And how the turtles just waved goodbye.

The gulls squawk loud, like they own the sky,
While starry-eyed minnows swim by, oh my!
"Is that breakfast?" they gawk in surprise,
But the chef is a catfish in a chef's disguise!

As morning winks and stretches wide,
The seaside laughs, with joy and pride.
In echoes of solitude, a giggle rings,
As life at dawn wears its funnier flings.

Fogbound Reverie

In the murky gloom we roam,
Chasing shadows, far from home.
Laughter echoes, soft and bright,
As we trip in absent light.

Lost my socks to the thick haze,
Mysterious games in this gray maze.
I ask the fog if it can see,
It replies with giggles, 'Let it be!'

Raindrops dance on my nose,
As I dodge a bush—who knows?
Every step's a guessing game,
In this hazy world, we're all the same.

Grinning banshees in the mist,
Whisper secrets of a twist.
Where is the path? Oh, what a plight,
Just follow laughter, it feels so right!

Silhouettes in Silence

The silhouettes sway, dance and play,
Waltzing softly, come what may.
I wave to folks who aren't quite there,
Did I just trip? Oh, what a scare!

Muffled chuckles fill the air,
Is it the fog, or just my hair?
I call out names, they sound like giggles,
But turn out to be just my wiggles.

Ghosts of trees seem to conspire,
With the night, they never tire.
One more step and look ahead,
Oh no! That was just my bed!

With ice cream cones that disappear,
Lost in whirlpools of sheer cheer.
We dance like fools, a merry band,
Swaying lightly, hand in hand!

Beneath the Gray Veil

Beneath a veil of fluffy white,
I lost my shoes on a silly flight.
Sandwiches float, like dreams untold,
The fog's a prankster, good as gold!

With every step, I hear a tune,
Is it a cat or maybe a loon?
The sun may hide, but I won't scowl,
We'll make our fun, no need to howl!

Sailing socks on a misty sea,
I wonder if they're laughing at me.
With pies in the sky and sprinkles on ground,
The fog grows thicker, joy unbound.

So onward we go, a merry crew,
Dropping giggles like morning dew.
In this thick fog, we'll surely bask,
In a world where we don't need to ask!

Ciphers of the Mist

In the thick of a puzzling haze,
I find my keys, or so it pays.
Green frogs leap with a wink or two,
Speaking riddles and jokes askew.

Up in the fog, a cat does sing,
Swishing its tail—what a funny thing!
A puzzle box, without a clue,
What secrets lie beneath the dew?

Every turn brings giggles near,
Fuzzy faces bloom with cheer.
Try to catch a bubble-shaped thought,
With whimsy's help, it can't be bought!

So let's embrace this misty play,
With laughter blooming all the way.
In ciphers strange, our joy will lift,
Amidst the fog, a wondrous gift!

Lost in the Brume

I wandered in a misty maze,
Where bright green frogs all sang and played.
A seagull swooped and stole my hat,
While I just stood and said, "Well, that's that!"

The trees did dance like drunken pals,
As fog embraced the cheeky gales.
I lost my way, but found a crab,
Who offered me a friendly jab.

A lighthouse blinked its goofy light,
All blink and no direction right.
I chased a shadow, lost my shoe,
And bumped my head on a kangaroo!

In this strange land where comedies bloom,
I'll take my time to find the room.
And when the sun breaks through the haze,
I'll laugh at all my foggy days.

A Glimpse of Solitude

A lonely rock marked my retreat,
With rubber ducks and one bare feat.
They floated past, not making sound,
In a sea of grey where joys abound.

With fish that giggled in their schools,
And jellybeans with lots of drools.
I tried to sit, enjoy the view,
But tripped on seaweed, oh so blue!

The wind decided it was a tease,
It tossed my snacks into the breeze.
I shouted at the waves, so bold,
"Bring back my chips!" they laughed and scrolled.

A squirrel claimed my picnic throne,
With acorn snacks that felt like stone.
In solitude, I found a crowd,
Of critters wearing hats so loud!

Enchanted by the Haze

In a whimsical haze, I lost my grip,
On a jellyfish that did a flip.
It wiggled and jiggled, went 'hey, look here!'
While I just laughed and sipped my beer.

The colors swirled like a painter's tease,
As wobbly ducks sailed in the breeze.
I joined a parade of giggling frogs,
Who led me right into some soggy logs.

"Where are the landmarks?" I asked aloud,
As seaweed waved like a mischievous crowd.
A fish retorted, "Stay in your lane!
This is all a part of our silly game!"

Laughter echoed through the murky air,
With bubble-blowers everywhere!
In my foggy funk, I found my glee,
Amidst the silliness, so wild and free.

Murmurs of the Sea Breeze

The whispers of the breeze did play,
As seagulls staged a funny ballet.
They twisted and twirled with flappy flair,
While I just stood, a curious bear.

The shells had stories, or so they claimed,
About the beach where mermaids aimed.
I asked for directions, they just sighed,
And spun a tale as I just pried.

With a wink, the waves would swipe my feet,
And tease me with their salty greet.
I danced along, a pause to tease,
With silly grains that made me wheeze.

In this breezy humor and sunny scorn,
I found my heart as light as dawn.
Through laughter and joy, the brume made me,
Realize where my spirit's free!

The Hidden Path

In the mist, I take a stroll,
Where the sea and sky console.
My left foot's in the brine,
While my right claims the pine.

A seagull squawks with glee,
Dressed as if it's me.
It's a fashion faux pas here,
Or perhaps I mishear!

Echoes in the Gloom

Whispers bounce off rocks we roam,
Is it the fog or my lost phone?
I chase voices in high glee,
While wondering if they're free.

A crab scuttles by in style,
Winking as it goes of a mile.
Does it mock my silly shoes?
Or does it have its own news?

Blurred Horizons

Shapes emerge in swirling haze,
But they dance in funny ways.
A ship? A caper? No one knows,
Except maybe the nearby crows.

They caw with laughter, what's their game?
Creating for me quite the fame.
As I trip on a playful log,
I become the star of this fog.

Lighthouses in the Grey

The beacon flickers with delight,
A lighthouse hoping to ignite.
"It's not my fault the ships are lost!"
"Get better bulbs!" it seems to toss.

I giggle at the light's despair,
While doing my foggy hair.
Who knew this mist could please,
And bring me to my knees!

Lullabies of the Tide

The seagulls squawk, a wild parade,
As crabs in pajamas refuse to wade.
A fish wearing glasses swims with glee,
While waves tell jokes, all wild and free.

The starfish dance in a clumsy way,
Singing off-key at the end of the day.
A whirlpool giggles, spins around,
While jellyfish drift, saying, "Look! I'm found!"

On sandy stages, the clams recite,
Their lines filled with puns, oh what a sight!
With each rising tide, a laugh or two,
The ocean's a stage, and we're all in view.

So when the sun sets with a wink and a glow,
The tide rolls away like a sitcom show.
And as we leave with smiles on our face,
The lullabies linger, a salty embrace.

The Eclipsed Shoreline

Where crabs play chess on a sandy shore,
And the tides are debating, a lively lore.
The gulls wear hats, a ridiculous sight,
While seaweed dances, twirls with delight.

The sun lost a game of peek-a-boo,
As dolphins played tag, a splashy crew.
The ocean chuckles, a jovial tide,
Hiding its treasures with antics of pride.

An oyster's joke goes right over the head,
As starfish compete in a flip-flop spread.
With shells as their podiums, they proudly boast,
Of underwater things and a jellyfish toast.

In twilight's glow, the horizon grins,
As all of the sandcastles measure their wins.
And laughter drifts high into the night sky,
A coastal comedy, no reason to sigh.

Phantoms in the Fog

In a misty maze, the crabs disappear,
Playing hide and seek, filled with cheer.
A ghost from the past, with a silly face,
Floats on its raft, finds a slow pace.

Foggy figures dance like lost balloons,
Laughing and giggling to watery tunes.
A lighthouse nods, with a lantern's blink,
As fish in top hats enjoy a little drink.

The turtles race with a comical flair,
While mermaids gossip, tossing their hair.
With wispy whispers, they tease the night,
And shadows shimmy, all out of sight.

But as dawn approaches, the laughter will fade,
The phantoms retreat, their fun has been played.
And in the morning, with sunbeams aglow,
We'll remember the laughter from the tales of the show.

A Chorus of Clouds

The clouds have formed a humorous band,
Playing notes with a breeze, oh so grand.
A sprinkle of laughter, a drizzle of fun,
While rainbows dance, under the sun.

Fluffy formations drift in a line,
Singing silly songs, it's like a soft wine.
As raindrops giggle, and puddles cheer,
They splash in the laughter, so crystal clear.

With every gust, the melodies sway,
A whimsical waltz, night turns to day.
And fog joins in with a shy little nod,
As the air fills with joy, none can be flawed.

So let's lean back and enjoy the show,
With a sky that sings, and winds that blow.
In the theater of nature, let's take our place,
A chorus of clouds, a smiling embrace.

Secrets Beneath the Gloom

In the shadows, a crab does dance,
With jiggly legs that call for a chance.
Whispers of seaweed tickle their knott,
As fish giggle hard at the band it's got.

Underwater peep shows, only for gnome,
A clam wearing glasses, reading a tome.
Secrets, they say, are buried in sand,
But all we find is a smelly old hand.

Panic in bubbles as the tide rolls in,
A sea cucumber plotting with a grin.
Octopuses juggling, what a fine scene,
While starfish get tangled in a seaweed machine.

The sandcastles wobble, they hardly hold still,
As waves sneak in like a playful thrill.
So here we gather, in laughter we bask,
Finding new stories in every sea-task.

Mists that Embrace

A fog rolled in, like it owned the place,
Hiding the seagulls with ridiculous grace.
They flap and they squawk, a comedic flight,
Crashing on boats in a most funny sight.

On the pier, a fisherman starts a rant,
His catch of the day? Just a sad little plant.
He swears it was big, a whale in disguise,
While a jellyfish giggles, just down by his thighs.

Sneaky little seals, with their playful tricks,
Steal all the clam's pearls, what a crew of slicks!
They hold a parade through the watery glade,
As the gulls squawk in envy, their plan goes unmade.

When mists start to part, we'll share the delight,
Recalling the laughter, oh, what a fine night.
So raise up a toast, to the fog and its schemes,
A world full of humor, where nothing's as it seems.

Lost Reflections

Staring at puddles, we find no regrets,
Just ducks in a row and their quirky sets.
They honk with a flair, wearing hats made of weeds,
Reflecting the chaos, fulfilling our needs.

Mirror like waters, a dancing old fool,
With a wink and a grin, saying, "Ain't I cool?"
The fish they applaud with dramatic flair,
Making waves in the laughter, a watery air.

Foggy mishaps, where shadows all blend,
A turtle's slow crawl, we think it'll end.
But puffins are laughing, they find it a game,
In a puddle of giggles, nothing's the same.

So come join the fun, in our happy parade,
Where silliness reigns and fears start to fade.
The world's but a mirror, it's all in good jest,
Lost in reflections, this life's a fun fest.

Between Whispers and Waves

Between the whispers, the ocean will shout,
"Who spilled the drinks?" Oh, what a clout!
Mermaids are chuckling in shimmering tails,
While dolphins perform in their comedic trails.

Gather 'round folks, there's a seabird dance,
With flapping wings and a clumsy prance.
They drop all their snacks, what a silly sight,
As the gulls swoop down for a feathery fight.

Pirates lost treasure? They just found a shoe,
With seaweed garnish, the finest of stew!
They laugh at their fate, what a grand, foolish crew,
Committing to chaos, what else could they do?

Between whispers and waves, where nonsense abounds,
We toast to the creatures, the joys they surround.
In this realm of humor, let's dive right in,
For life's all a jest, let the giggles begin!

The Lost Coast

A pirate's map made of jelly beans,
Leads to treasure filled with canned sardines.
With a compass made of old gum and string,
We laugh at the silly fortunes it may bring.

The seagulls squawk their drunken song,
As we trip on rocks we don't belong.
Each splash a giggle, a slip, a fall,
Maybe we'll find gold, or just a wall.

The tide pulls back our dreams of fame,
Only to leave us playing a silly game.
With every wave a new blunder to greet,
Our journey's a mess, but we can't be beat.

So raise your flippers, your straws, your hats,
We'll toast to our luck with a can of gnats!
Adventure awaits, just around the bend,
What happens next? Well, it's hard to pretend.

Murky Wanderings

In a mist that swallows the shore,
I lost my shoes and maybe more.
As I search for signs in this thick old haze,
I find instead, a crab that plays.

With each lost step I find new friends,
A jellyfish has jokes—it never ends!
The fog is thick but the laughter is loud,
Together we dance, a strange little crowd.

The lighthouses wink at our silly plight,
Guiding misfits, both day and night.
"Just follow the giggles," the sea breeze rhymes,
We'll navigate through, one laugh at a time.

The stars above are shy tonight,
But we'll be fine, it feels so right.
So onward we frolic, in search of more,
In murky wanderings, adventure's the core.

Reflections in the Fog

In dreamy grey, the world does peek,
We search for treasure, so unique.
A mirror of silliness dances in sight,
As we chase our laughter, dodging the bite.

The waves snicker softly, plotting their pranks,
While we spend hours acting like flanks.
With every twist, my hat takes a dive,
"Hey! Come back!" I shout, "you can't just thrive!"

Reflections ripple through foggy airs,
Creating mermaids with curious glares.
They giggle and float, tossing us shells,
We join in their chorus, spinning our spells.

Adventure's our game, silliness our guide,
With fog as our cloak, we take it in stride.
So should you pass, don't take us too keen,
For we're all just reflections—part silly, part sheen.

The Art of Abandon

I left my jacket on a beachy throne,
Where sandcastles flourish and seagulls moan.
But the tide giggles softly, taking it away,
As I ponder my choices in the sunny fray.

The art of letting go, I soon understand,
Is like losing a snack to an ambitious hand.
So I chase the waves with a silly cheer,
And embrace the mess of this windy frontier.

With sunglasses crooked and hair like a broom,
I dance with a dolphin, in this foggy gloom.
Together we frolic, mischief our muse,
Creating a show that's bound to amuse.

So here's to the whimsies in every direction,
To the lost little treasures, the joyful dissection!
Life is a canvas where laughter's the paint,
In the art of abandon, we become the quaint.

Gateways to the Unknown

A door creaks slow, then swings wide,
Inside, a parrot plays the guide,
With feathers bright and tales so tall,
He squawks and dances, heed my call.

Around the bend, a sign appeared,
"Beware of ghosts!" I surely feared.
But cats in capes just pranced about,
Laughing softly, filled with clout.

A treasure map, all scribbled lines,
Leads me to pancakes, sweet like wines.
The pirates here are chefs it seems,
With buttered gold and syrup dreams.

So if you seek a bizarre delight,
Take a chance; don't skip the flight.
For every step, a joke unfolds,
In laughter's grip, our fate beholds.

The Embrace of Silence

The quiet's thick, like peanut cream,
In every corner, whispers scheme.
A snail debates its post on rocks,
While crabs knit hats from fishing socks.

Beneath a tree, a gopher sighs,
While squirrels play poker, full of lies.
The stillness hums a silly song,
That keeps the owls awake too long.

I hear a cough, is it a ghost?
Or just the wind, its icy boast?
A turtlenecked seal gives me a wink,
And laughs so hard, it starts to sink.

The peace we sought, it plays the fool,
With every giggle breaking the rule.
Embrace the quiet, but not too tight,
For silly secrets dance at night.

Echoes of Distant Shores

The waves crash loud like a toddler's fight,
While gulls recite their poems of plight.
A fish with glasses swims past me,
Waving hello, "It's like TV!"

From shells, I hear an opera sing,
As crabs in tuxes do their thing.
"Encore! Encore!" the mermaids cheer,
But only the seaweed can hear.

A pirate's map, upside down,
Leads straight to a wobbly town.
There, a king sits wearing flip-flops,
Proclaiming, "All hail pizza pops!"

With echoes soft, the laughter swells,
As seagulls spin their yarns and yells.
Distant shores, with humor abound,
Leave giggles floating all around.

Shimmering Secrets

Beneath the waves, a disco ball,
Fish in tuxedos, heed the call.
They shimmy-shake in swirling mist,
While jellyfish dance like they're kissed.

A treasure chest with socks inside,
And coins that giggle while they hide.
A crab with shades, he takes my hand,
Says, "Join our funky underwater band!"

Seashells whisper, "Tell us a joke!"
While dolphins laugh until they croak.
They ride the waves, they twist and twirl,
In a surf of sparkles, give it a whirl!

Shimmering secrets in every splash,
As fishes fly in an acrobatic dash.
So join the fun, don't hesitate,
In ocean's heart, we celebrate!

Soft Embrace of Twilight

As daylight fades, the crabs convene,
Clawing their way to a show unseen.
Whispers of laughter ride on the breeze,
While seagulls squawk their evening tease.

A fish in a suit, with tie and a hat,
Joined a dance with a cheeky old cat.
They twirled on the sand, what a sight to see,
A crustacean party, quite wild and free!

Under the stars that twinkle and shine,
The sea sings sweet songs with saucy design.
While shadows creep, tickling toes on the shore,
The night keeps us giggling, who could ask for more?

So let's raise a toast to the weird and the fun,
To crabs, cats, and fish, all under the sun.
In twilight's embrace where silliness reigns,
We'll dance till the tide comes to wash out our stains.

Driftwood Dreams

A piece of driftwood with tales to weave,
Sat dreaming of mermaids, hard to believe.
With twinkling shells as jewelry made,
Thanks to the tide for this charming parade.

A jellyfish in boots, what a sight to see,
Strolled by with a grin, oh so fancy-free.
"Let's start a conga," it wiggled with glee,
The starfish chimed in, "Join in, follow me!"

Bottles floated by with messages vague,
One asked for a drink, another a leg.
They all had their quirks, oh how they would clash,
While driftwood dreamers threw a beachy bash!

So raise up your glasses of salty brine,
To the whimsical wonders where laughter's divine.
For in the blues where the sea creatures play,
Every driftwood dancer has something to say!

Gossamer at Sea

A spider on board, knitting nets of delight,
Claimed it caught seaweed but lost it that night.
With shimmer and shine, the waves did reflect,
Fish giggled aloud, "Is it us to protect?"

The boat swayed gently, a scene quite absurd,
As octopuses waved, lost in their word.
One missed the party, squinting through a glass,
"Did I miss the boat?" they pondered with sass.

Kites danced on the water, fish flapping their fins,
Dolphins donned glasses, declaring their wins.
With every splash, a chorus would rise,
"Sea life is wild! Oh what a surprise!"

So let's toast to the mischief found in the tides,
To the gossamer dreams where the funny resides.
In the frothy blue, with laughter as fuel,
We'll sail on together, but don't lose the school!

Dreams Carried by Mist

A fog rolled in, wearing a top hat too wide,
With whispers and giggles, it danced by the tide.
"Have you seen my sock?" a clam cried in fright,
It laughed as it shimmered, fading from sight.

Selkies in flippers played leapfrog with glee,
While seagulls debated how to dive free.
"Your aim is all wrong!" one called with a grin,
As fish swam below in a raucous din.

The lighthouse laughed loud, its beam flashed with cheer,

Leading lost boats back, while drinking a beer.
And mist swirled around, making dance steps anew,
With dreams interwoven, a fun rendezvous.

So here's to the laughter that wraps us so tight,
In cloudy confusions, from morning till night.
When the shoreline calls out with jokes in the air,
We'll follow the mist, with our hearts laid bare!

Ephemeral Whispers

In the morning haze, I tripped on my shoe,
Chasing seagulls who laughed, just one or two.
They stole my sandwich, or maybe it's fate,
Now I just wave, and watch them dictate.

A crab in a tux said, "Do come join me!"
As he danced on the sand, all wild and free.
The waves were his partner, he twirled with glee,
I laughed so hard, my lunch turned to brie.

A pelican swooped, with a wink and a grin,
"Don't worry, my friend, you can't lose with skin!"
He dropped a whole fish, right next to my hat,
I wore it with pride, though my hair looked like that.

Then a dolphin appeared, with a splash and a flip,
"Want to race, my friend? Take a dip! Take a dip!"
We dashed through the water, what fun we all had,
Who knew in the fog, being silly was rad?

Dreams in the Mist.

Napping on the shore, I dreamt of a whale,
He wore a top hat, and spoke without fail.
"Good day, dear friend, care for a ride?"
I said, "Only if your tuxedo is wide!"

The mist swirled around, like a playful sprite,
A sea otter appeared, oh what a sight!
"Join me for tea in my cozy shell café,
But watch out for crabs, they might steal your tray!"

I followed the otter, dodging slimy snails,
We danced past the clams, and we laughed without fails.
With each soggy cookie, we snickered and cheered,
Who knew underwater could be so weird?

But suddenly, fog turned thicker and thick,
"Where are we?" I asked, feeling quite sick.
"I think we're lost!" said my friend with a snort,
"Let's just make tea and not worry for sport!"

Whispers of the Hidden Shore

The tide whispered secrets, the shells broke the news,
That crabs hold the gossip, while sunbathers snooze.
I listened intently, with a wink and a grin,
As the barnacles chattered, "Let the fun begin!"

A jellyfish danced, with a wobbly flair,
He invited the starfish for a weightless affair.
"Come on, do the jig, don't get stuck in the muck,
Just don't tell the seagulls, they'll ruin our luck!"

They flapped and they flopped, with a shriek and a squawk,
Dressed up in feathers, like some fashion mock.
I tried to keep serious, but lost to the jokes,
In the fog, all the waves became giggling folks!

So I joined their big party, with laughter so loud,
In a world of absurdity, we danced in the crowd.
The ocean's my friend, waving bright and content,
It's a silly kind of joy, that's pleasantly bent.

Veils of Mystery in the Mist

In a misty lagoon, there lurked a large fish,
He promised to grant me a whimsical wish.
"Wanna fly, little buddy?" he winked with a grin,
"Just hop on my back, and let the fun begin!"

We soared through the clouds, or maybe just fog,
Hand in fin, like a fairytale cog.
A pirate ship sailed, with a parrot so bright,
"Join us for treasure! We'll dance 'til the night!"

But my fish friend shouted, "We must make a stop,
The waves need our talent, not just slow bop!"
And down we descended, like a splashy delight,
As a chorus of dolphins began to ignite.

They sang silly songs, making waves to the beat,
With seaweed confetti, oh, what a treat!
In the end, I awoke, with sand in my hair,
Dreams in the mist, filled with laughter and flair.

Silken Threads of a Shrouded Journey

In the mist, I lost my way,
Chasing shadows of disarray.
A seagull laughed, my compass broke,
My map unfurled, and then I spoke.

A crab with swagger crossed my path,
He wiggled, danced, then sparked a laugh.
With not a clue, I stepped ahead,
To find the snacks I thought I'd shed.

Fog said, "Where'd your sandwich go?"
I answered back, "You should know!"
But mysteries grew like the sea foam,
As I stumbled on this aquatic roam.

Yet in this haze, I felt so light,
Like a dizzy fool in morning light.
For under layers of fluffy grey,
Laughter echoed, leading the way.

The Heartbeat of a Fog-Wrapped World

With each step, a squish and splat,
I wondered where the pathways sat.
The air was thick, the silence loud,
A penguin waved, called me a crowd.

Mist rolled in with secrets fawned,
As I, in giggles, only yawned.
Tripping over invisible roots,
While sea cucumbers wore small boots!

A lighthouse flickered with delight,
Saying, "Get lost, you'll be alright!"
But fog was thick and clouds would tease,
As I dodged waves and climbed the breeze.

The world was wrapped in whims and snorts,
As seals played tricks like playful sports.
In this wobbly, foggy embrace,
I found my joy in this silly place.

Murky Depths and Unseen Shores

Diving deep into thickened air,
I bumped my head, oh my, beware!
A shimmering fish just winked at me,
"Join the fun!" it said, "Come see!"

The seaweed tangled in bright green knots,
Chasing bubbles and seeing spots.
A whale's giggle rippled the sea,
While decoy boats went 'Whee!' with glee.

I tripped on a conch, its shell was grand,
And found a treasure chest made of sand.
But when I peeked, my heart did froth,
It held old socks - not gold, just cloth!

Yet joy is found in funny blunders,
As waves crash down with silly thunders.
In these vague realms where laughter rolls,
I danced with joy, and freed my souls.

The Solace of Wandering in the Grey

In a sleepy world where shadows sway,
I bumbled along in shades of gray.
A duck quacked loudly, "Give me a break!"
I chuckled back, "Let's eat some cake!"

The fog was thick, but we pressed on,
With giggles making spirits drawn.
I fancied a feast on a marshmallow cloud,
As foggy whispers cheered aloud.

An octopus sought to share its tea,
Its cups were shells, as cute as can be.
I spilled a bit on a passing fish,
It splashed back, granting my wish!

In the grey, I found silly glee,
With friends unseen, they welcomed me.
As laughter bloomed, the fog did part,
And joy emerged to fill the heart.

Beneath the Wisp of Foggy Skies

The seagulls squawk in a muffled breeze,
I misplace my sandwich, oh what a tease!
A pelican lands, steals my last fry,
Laughing, we wave as it roams by.

With whispers of sea and laughter so light,
We dance on the pier, what a sight,
The fog rolls in like an old friend's hug,
While tripping on driftwood, we laugh and shrug.

A crab takes a stroll, in a sideways jig,
He's dressed up splendid, oh so big!
Lost in a world of blurry delight,
Together we giggle, fading from sight.

In this wisp of wonder, all's a bit hazy,
The sun peeks through, but we're feeling crazy,
So let's toss our worries into the bay,
And dance with the fog till the end of the day.

Silhouettes of Ancient Tales in Vapor

There's a dog in a hat, quite a funny sight,
Chasing after shadows, with all of his might.
With whispers of legends, a pirate's code,
We laugh with the echoes down this foggy road.

A man in a cloak waves a plastic sword,
Claiming he's captain, oh what a horde!
The fog plays tricks on our eager minds,
As we seek out treasure, the best that we find.

A squirrel, a bard, with acorns galore,
Sings silly songs that we can't help but adore.
Together we stumble, our tales intertwine,
In this misty expanse, laughter's divine!

With figures that dance through the ghostly air,
We create our own tales, whimsical and rare.
So let's toast to the fog, strange and sublime,
As we wade through the tales, giggling all the time.

Wandering Souls in the Shifting Mists

We wander carefreely, while cloaked in gray,
Finding lost marbles from games gone astray.
The lighthouse blinks slowly, a guide from afar,
Reminding us all just how weird we are.

Mysterious whispers, like echoes of cheer,
Floating on fog, can anyone hear?
A fish in a bowler hat jumps and croaks,
And the laughter erupts from all of our jokes.

Through shimmers of light, and shadows that peep,
We share all the secrets that we all keep.
In this hazy embrace, we twirl and we spin,
With giggles and grins, so much joy within.

So let's skip through the mist, hand in hand,
Chasing the giggles like grains of sand.
Each step is a dance, each laugh is a key,
Unlocking the joy, just you and me.

Love Letters Scattered in the Gloom

A message in a bottle, right in the weeds,
Faced with our giggles, it just brings us needs.
With glances exchanged, and hearts all a-flutter,
We'll read each sweet note, whilst playing in clutter.

A foggy embrace, a dance in the night,
Where shadows are silly, and laughter feels right.
With letters like treasures, all misplaced,
We're searching through dreams, not a moment to waste.

In the misty unknown, our love finds a place,
Wrapped up in giggles, the perfect embrace.
With hearts like balloons, floating on air,
We're lost in the lovely, beyond any care.

So gather the letters, let's chuckle and play,
Each line a small secret, we'll treasure today.
Amid swirling fog, we'll find our sweet bloom,
In this soft, silly world, where love finds its room.

Lanterns of Hope in the Murk

Blinky lights above the marsh,
Wobbling like they've had too much to drink,
Chasing ducks that quack and splash,
Wondering what's wrong with the stink.

A lone seal pops up to say,
"I lost my way, can you lend a paw?"
Underwater fun turned gone astray,
Now he's just a fishy law.

The moon plays peekaboo all night,
With shadows dancing, twist and twirl,
Jellyfish float with glittering light,
Doing the tango, what a whirl!

In the fog, laughter hangs in the air,
Seagulls squawking like they run the show,
Even the crabs have got flair,
Strutting sideways like they know where to go.

The Last Light Before the Cloak

A flicker in the distance shines,
Like the fortune teller's crystal ball,
Is it a lighthouse or the neighbor's signs?
Maybe it's just a snoopy cat, after all!

Footprints lead to a squishy patch,
Where puddles double as trampoline farms,
Leap ahead, then take a scratch,
Someone just lost their favorite charms!

Miracles in the marsh, quite absurd,
Frogs reciting poetry quite bizarre,
Each croak ringing clear, every word,
Brought giggles to moonlit stars.

So led by light, we tiptoe through,
In search of laughs and maybe a snack,
Puns and giggles, we pursue,
Trust the glow, or do we turn back?

A Journey Beyond Sight's Embrace

Wobbly boats on water's edge,
Paddles swing like they're playing hockey,
"Is this the path?" we wonder and hedge,
Our guide is a raccoon, slightly cocky!

Soggy sandwiches swim about,
As the seagulls laugh in overhead prance,
Crumbs creating quite the hoot and shout,
"For us? Don't mind if we chance!"

Turtles sunbathing, wearing sun hats,
They say they've seen a real live ghost,
Turns out it's just some old field rats,
Trying to barbecue bread for a toast.

We stumble on, through thick and thin,
Fog hides the path in a fluffy hug,
But laughter bubbles up from within,
As we dodge the sneaky old sludge.

Whispers of the Past in the Mist

In the haze, voices twisted,
"Did you hear about Fred the fish?"
He's been back and forth, unassisted,
Stealing bait, that naughty swish!

Fiddly creatures spin tales so tall,
Of mermaids with bright neon lights,
They dance 'round the feet of the sprawl,
Just a decoy for cheeky delights!

The fog wraps secrets, crafty and sly,
Like grandma's quilt draped on a chair,
Though whispers fade and giggles fly,
What's a bit of mischief to share?

So let's get lost in giggles and whim,
As the mist keeps our spirits alight,
With every chuckle, we dance on a whim,
In the twilight fog, we'll be alright.

Enigmatic Shores of the Nebulous Sea

Waves whisper secrets, they can't quite keep,
Jellyfish giggle as they drift and weep.
Seagulls wear shades, playing fashionista,
While clams drop the beat in a weird fiesta.

Sandcastles tumble, a thump and a splash,
With invisible seashells, they make quite a bash.
Who needs a map when the fog's your guide?
Just follow the sound of the sand crab's slide.

A pirate appears, but just in your head,
He's searching for treasure, or maybe some bread.
With fog as his cloak and a wink in his eye,
He gestures for fish, but they're just passing by.

So here on the shores, the disaster is fun,
Where lost socks abound and the sun's shy to run.
The sea sings a tune, while we dance on the sand,
Laughing like fools, it's a whimsical land.

The Dance of Gulls in Low Visibility

Gulls flap their wings in a chaotic ballet,
Missing the wind, they drift where they may.
With twirls and bright squawks, they launch a parade,
While fish roll their eyes, in the dark they stay laid.

In this bowl of grays, the comedy flows,
Birds crashing mid-air, where nobody knows.
Their landing's a mess, a real slapstick scene,
As the sun peeks through, looking hot in between.

A crab waves his claw, joins in their dance,
He's got crumply moves with a pinch of romance.
Gulls laugh at the sight, then swirl out of reach,
While the starfish stares on, stuck up on the beach.

With a flourish, they bow to the great ocean blue,
Another failed landing, but they're loving the view.
In a haze of absurdity, they strut and they chatter,
As fog rolls away, who cares? It's all that matters.

Twilight Tales of the Obscured Bay

Bats flit like shadows, with zero finesse,
While crabs tell tall tales, of boldness no less.
The lighthouse yawns wide, shrouded in mist,
As the moon snickers softly, 'We just can't resist!'

Fish gossip below about the evening's plans,
Complaining of fog that hides their sun tans.
"Last week I was spotted! It was quite the thrill,
But tonight's just a whisper, and I'm feeling quite ill."

A mermaid shows up, in a cloak of gray haze,
With a wink and a smile, she's setting the phase.
"Join me for singsongs 'neath stars, oh-so-faint,
Grab a crab on your way and don't be a saint!"

So forth they go wandering, mischief in tow,
Creating new tales in the dimming aglow.
With giggles and guffaws, they haunt like a cloud,
In this silly, strange world, they dance way too loud.

Murmurs from the Fogbound Forest

Trees giggle together, their branches entwined,
As squirrels trade secrets, all silly and blind.
Fog swirls around, like a game of peek-a-boo,
While owls hoot "No pics!" and ducks quack "Who knew?"

A raccoon in boots tries to strut like a star,
But tripping on twigs, he won't get too far.
"That's not how you moonwalk," a porcupine sighs,
As he rolls in the leaves, no truth in his lies.

Mushrooms are giggling, their colors so bright,
They throw a small rave beneath the pale light.
With fireflies twinkling, like stars in updrafts,
They move to the beat, while the forest just laughs.

So if you wander in, through the silliness framed,
You'd hear all the chuckles wherein nature's tamed.
In a world full of wonder, you can't help but grin,
For the fog bounds the laughter, let the fun begin!

www.ingramcontent.com/pod-product-compliance
Lightning Source LLC
Chambersburg PA
CBHW072221070526
44585CB00015B/1430